Gospel Midrashim

Gospel Midrashim

Poems on the Life of Jesus

KEN BAZYN

RESOURCE *Publications* · Eugene, Oregon

GOSPEL MIDRASHIM
Poems on the Life of Jesus

Resource Publications
An Imprint of Wipf and Stock Publishers
199 W. 8th Ave., Suite 3
Eugene, OR 97401
www.wipfandstock.com

ISBN 13: 978-1-62032-797-5

Manufactured in the U.S.A.

To the Chelsea United Methodist Church,
where I grew up and was nurtured

Contents

Preface

Am I Inspired?

I sit diligently in my study
though the Muses are bored
and gossip rudely about my snobbish intentions.

Acknowledgments

SPECIAL THANKS TO MY wife, Barbara, for the full range of meaningful questions she posed concerning my poems and to David Reynolds for the careful stylistic and theological issues he raised while copyediting and computer formatting.

Thanks also go to the publications in which the following poems appeared:
"The Letter" in *Colonnades*
"Consider the Lilies" in *Crux*
"Lift Up Your Drooping Knees" in *C.S. P. World News*
"Exponential Sin" in *International Poetry Quarterly*

Introduction

Symbolic Acts

"Make Christ the only goal of your life. Dedicate to him all your enthusiasm, all your effort, your leisure as well as your business. And don't look upon Christ as a mere word, an empty expression, but rather as charity, simplicity, patience, and purity."[1]

—DESIDERIUS ERASMUS

JESUS IS THE PRIMARY role model for all Christian behavior. By immersing ourselves in the Gospels, we learn more about what he said, did, and thought. Broad-minded souls like nineteenth-century Transcendentalist Ralph Waldo Emerson took sharp exception to this "noxious exaggeration about the *person* of Jesus," preferring instead, to borrow from traditions outside Christianity and to follow the infinite law within: "The soul knows no persons. It invites every man to expand to the full circle of the universe, and will have no preferences but those of spontaneous love."[2]

Jesus, however, is the life-changer par excellence. "I will show you him that was a lion till then, and is now a lamb;" shouted John Wesley, "him that was a drunkard, and is now exemplarily sober;

1. Erasmus, *Handbook of the Militant Christian*, 58.
2. Emerson, "An Address," 54-55.

the whoremonger that was, who now abhors the very 'garment spotted by the flesh.'"[3] In Christ new impulses start to bubble up; old sinful habits subside. Thus, in his letter to the Ephesians, Paul urged former thieves to make an honest living and to share what they earn with those in need (Eph. 4:28). What a turnaround!

In every age and in every conceivable manner, Jesus turns lives upside down. Commenting on painter/engraver Albrecht Dürer's acceptance of the teachings of Martin Luther, art historian Erwin Panofsky writes that there was a "conversion—both in subject matter and in style." This man "who had done more than any other to familiarize the Northern world with the true spirit of pagan Antiquity now practically abandoned secular subject matter except for scientific illustrations, traveler's records and portraiture." Instead, Dürer chose to concentrate on religious images as of the evangelists, apostles, and Christ's own passion—moving from a decorative style to a more three-dimensional, "cubistic" one.[4]

In the Four Gospels Jesus' life is vividly etched in by a series of such symbolic acts as turning water into wine; healing the sick and lepers; casting out demons; calling the twelve; sending out the seventy; feeding the five thousand; teaching in parables; cleansing the temple; raising Lazarus from the dead; entering Jerusalem in triumph during Passover; washing the feet of the disciples; holding a last meal; willingly suffering an ignominious death. By conveying God's message in acts supercharged with meaning, Jesus followed in a long line of prophets. Jeremiah wore a yoke around his neck (Jer. 27:1–11); Isaiah walked about "naked" and barefoot (Isa. 20:1–5); Ezekiel sketched a diagram of Jerusalem onto a brick and constructed miniature siege works (Ezek. 4:1–3); Moses performed signs and wonders before Pharaoh (Exod. 7–12); Hosea married a whore (Hos. 1:1–8).

It is clear that we must heed not only prophetic words, but deeds. Church history is also filled to overflowing with countless instances of saints who have confronted the world through all manner of faith-filled antics which challenged the prevailing order. Such

3. Wesley, *The Journal of the Rev. John Wesley*, 202.
4. Panofsky, *The Life and Art of Albrecht Dürer*, 199–200.

acts can serve as templates for what we mortals may hope to accomplish in Jesus' name.

Let us then attend to both Jesus' words *and* deeds with reverence and awe. May we more fully fathom the significance of all he said and did, letting it take root in our everyday lives. May his speech *and* actions be an artesian well for our confused and wandering souls, infusing all we say and do with their truth and meaning. My poems are loosely arranged around his exceptional life. The footnotes point to scriptures to aid you in meditation.

Holding Back [1]

Always holding back,
afraid of the quiver in God's compass.

The Crystal Incarnation[2]

"Fiorito è Cristo nella carne pura."
—JACOPONE DA TODI[3]

In the crystal incarnation
  vials of heaven-sent fragrance
wrapped in satin
  are now tinctured red.

Purity within a transparent container
  envelops burst Godhead,
the new wine stretches the old skins
  into a bruised, malefactor form.

Humankind grows weary
  of this Lao-tzu of epigram,
regal splendor reborn
  in an unkempt stable.

With no golden midwives
  or earthly crown jewels
to remember him by.
  The most sublime the universe knows

Is now crying in a lowly manger where
  scruffy, ignorant shepherds keep watch,
the one to whom all praise is due
  is hunted by Herod's blackguard,

2. John 1:14.
3. Kay, *"De la incarnazione del verbo divino,"* 13.

Flees death-squads and firstborn threats
   until a safer, more seasonable time,
a volatile, incendiary experiment
   still mocked by scholars:

To enflesh newborn innocence
   in a tousled carpenter's robe,
to feel Satan's temptations—full blast—
   in this, our new covenant Job.

To set a meteor burning,
   whose embers shall warmly glow
in winter's debilitating clime
   on this water-blue bright planet.

A representative zoomorph
   of incommunicable joys,
who summons Aladdin's lamp
   for the believing child

In all of us.

He Came Among Us at Christmastide[4]

In frigid December
when the mercury froze,
the snow howled around our thermal underwear,
Venus set and Saturn was begotten from Jesse's shoot,
the Godhead fluttering as primate man.

Shepherds tooting their double-pipes,
Chaldean astrologers plotting horoscopes,
God hovering about this charred race,
angelic Yuletide a cappella,
stoop before thy Davidic seat.

Mary's hothouse incubator
gestating till the giant's a double nature,
handmaid of the *nephilim*,
all flesh shall see Christmas
draped in a plywood stall.

A gift-wrapped Immanuel
—red, black, brown, and Caucasian—
gurgling planets, a snow-white ermine
soaked red on Calvary's bark.

An apprehensive father, a midwife's stupor,
the labor of omnipotence,
Persian cologne, myrrh from Petra,
a 24-carat jewel of a boy,
the bulk of Esias's visions.

4. Luke 2:7.

Incarnate gums sucking Mary's teats,
a spotless manchild among steers and mules,
Bethlehem's first station on Lenten fourteen,
a Pax Brittanica befitting
the Prince of Calm.

A peppermint pacifier and a glittering ball of hope,
Mithra's birthday usurped
by Moses's gushing rock,
a winter solstice eve
broken up by a Twelfth-Night thaw.

The Magi[5]

With their Phrygian caps and astrolabes,
one-humped dung camels,
Babylonian liverectomies,
they stop. Ask Herod for directions?

Like gilded red-footed boobies,
they give off an impressionistic halation.
The gaping clowns, jugglers, and acrobats
heehaw at oneiromantic triangulation,
Gentile monarchs prostrate before that diapered Jew?

Bar Kokba genealogies,
Caspar's gold, Balthazar's frankincense, Melchior's myrrh,
Joseph the Uranoscopidae?
I'm not fit to bear his handkerchief
and is he my ambient Apelles?

All depart via some donkey cart route,
take trophy Pyrrhus's toe,
veiled in darkness they return to their Towers of Silence,
millenarian Amida Buddhists.

5. Matthew 2:1–2.

In an Enclosed Garden[6]

God, must pain birth forth you, my Lord?
wise old astrologers ponder inscrutable questions,
  dancing stars, seraph arias,
  shepherds shall lead us in praise.
O little town of Israel,
like Muslims we touch our heads to the sand,
am I the handmaiden to the *Ruach Hakodesh*?
  Messiah dangling from my umbilical cord
  like a blood offering to the skies.

The Virgin Queen playing a virginal tune,
Joseph on ukulele,
  the whole earth's a band of gold
  and we're the Benedictus and the Magnificat.
In the dice games of Demeter
the king alternately wins or loses,
the weaving of Penelope is unraveled every morning,
  so the kingdom of Jesus
  comes *piano e forte.*

From an enclosed garden the rose of Sharon springs,
speculum sine macula chained to a pomegranate tree.
  Tempted at the pinnacle,
  he threw caution at Pilate's seat,
unimpeded by conception,
he races forward, Paschal agonizing
  —the philosophers, dazzled and annoyed—
  does even his mother perceive his goal?

6. Luke 1:30–31.

The Homage of Herod[7]

Here, baby Jesus,
I have a present, too,
which hand:
the ruby sword or the carnelian dagger?

7. Matthew 2:7–8, 16–18.

The Letter[8]

God mailed the earth a letter,
he sealed it with *eau de cologne*,
Gabriel delivered it in a millisecond,
it fell open in Mary's fallopian tubes.

His signature was so illegible,
It took thirty years to decipher,
some snickered, a few chortled, most lent him no ear,
crumpled it up in their pockets
or sent it back in disgust.

8. John 1:11.

Let Not Sin . . . [9]

Let not sin reign within your mortal frames
nor be subject to its demonic twists and vicissitudes,
yield rather to Paraclete promptings, unequivocal charisms;
instead of being enamored by terrestrial baubles and gems,
allow no deep-seated dominion over your trenchant faculties,
for an idol is shaped by whatever you're dream-attached.

Be dead unto vice and alive unto continuous effacement,
having subdued the old, haughty, self-indulgent man,
stifled the duplicitous heart, rewired the punitive brain;
present your bodies as a living holocaust
on an altar misshapen by guilt-dripping hands,
relighting embers via Pentecostal bellows and blasts.

I am not now what I can nor should be,
nor anywhere near to what I shall become,
so I push forward with an unsteady, seesaw gait,
renewed and transfigured by ever more glorious images,
till the buried likeness of Christ be revealed
and I form an unassuming *exemplum* or *figura* of home.

From the tranquil, sanctified, melodious center,
I strive mightily to view life from the inverse end
    of the Gospel scope,
tripping wires, bursting straitjackets,
till I mirror all that's of eternal consequence,
forsaking not my high, upward call
by twaddling about in puddles or mired in insipid pools.

I must decrease, but Thou must encroach to encompass all.

9. John 3:30.

The Kingdom of Heaven[10]

The kingdom of heaven is like a thimble,
small enough to prick yourself on.

10. Luke 10:8–9.

Providence[11]

Yonder are your flora and fauna,
the wombat and the ruffed grouse,
Tyrannosaurus and Leviathan,
myriad creatures, both great and small,
look up to Providence
as I depend on Caesar.

All things float down from the arms of God
in love's cryptogram—
bones, flesh, arteries and intelligence—
in a Pentecostal flourish or the leanness of Elijah's years.

Each prays in an unknown tongue,
throws his minted coins in the cup,
each blesses, and in turn, receives a benediction,
one rejoices with robust aplomb, another is more inhibited,
one sinks down ecstatically,
a brother claps his hands in praise.

All form golden silkworm threads,
all sup of the Eucharistic basin,
all partake of pure, unending life,
all serve their neighbors with simple grace.

You, the almighty potentate,
spinner of universes, peace-loving Elizabeth,
author of concord,
in your secret chest lie treasures hid,
at your right hand joy and temperance kiss,
on your lap all dreams ring true.

11. Matthew 5:45.

Fantasies and adventures to spoil Don Quixote's quest,
riches to o'ershadow the earring Cleopatra drank.
If heaven's flood gate op'd wide,
you'd swamp us all;
meanwhile, we cling like unripe seed
on your voluptuous vine.

What Manner of Man Is This?[12]

What manner of man is this
that the winds and the sea
obey his minuscule voice?
Demoniacs seal their doom;
infirmities vanish
as if from under an evil spell.
Samaritans flock like ripening grain
to a well which mirrors sin;
centurions give and receive salutes,
march to a different fife and drummer.

Like a giant who stands above, he disputes Moses,
flaunting the tradition of the elders
with a prophetic, "But I say unto you";
gathers tax collectors, zealots, unlettered fishermen
into his innermost circle of twelve;
calls God, "My Father";
speaks of heaven—as if he'd seen the place;
answers trapdoor, leading questions
with penetrating, two-edged aphorisms.

A man merciful to thieves;
silent before his false accusers
and those with the power to save his earthly life;
reviling not those Caesaro-papist pretenders
who spit in his eye;
submitting to Joseph, Mary, the Baptist;
clarifying his teaching
with foot-washing *exempla*;
showing compassion on the sheep who wandered off
and ate of the poisonous weeds.

12. Matthew 8:27.

Those who seek him with a transparent heart,
he promises a portion of his persecutions,
plus a peepshow of uninterrupted companionship.

No Son of Mine[13]

If he asks for an egg, will you give him a scorpion?
If you retrieve his ball, will you bring him a hand grenade?
    David entered into Bathsheba,
    Absalom got hung up on a tree limb,
No son of mine shall feel the light undeflected.

Never at a loss, like some Turk strutting out the womb—
    yet Zagreus was ambushed by Titans
    with bullroarer toys and knucklebones,
    Joseph was camel-traded under Reuben's aegis,
    Esau tricked by his mother's broth—
this, my beloved son, was not nursed for infamy.

Out of the East ride three tall strangers
with scabbards, scythes and .38 caliber Gatling guns.
    My son grapples with the courage of Telemachus,
    trumpets the harsh words of Zebedee's boys,
    he, my cradled one, my little league grandslammer,
    despite himself, walks with the old man's
        lopsided gait:

The same receding forehead,
  more gallantry than poise,
    every gene pulling for intelligence,
      a paltry altruism.
Will my faults be exorcised so kindly,
my gaps filled in, closed?
Then spot me twenty years and spin off a sequel.

---

13. Luke 11:11–12.

A Hilarious Giver[14]

The Lord loves a hilarious giver,
frolicking in the aisles, jingling-
pocketed Mexican jumping beans,
popcorn celebrators, who can pull out
the widow's mite faster than Doc Holliday,
sprinkle alms among the needy,
like at Philippi fling freewill
toasts to Paul and Silas,
dispatch promissory notes for disasters,
strap themselves on the altar first—
then the coins flow freely,
hide their treasures in fire-proof,
mugger-proof, termite-proof vaults,
watch the dimes mature a hundredfold,
burden down the ushers with paper gratitude—
might require a crane at the blessing,

Stewards who plant the Gospel seed
despite the cockleburs,
iconoclasts sprung from lucre's grip,
airy, sanguine, mountain-pushers,
give not offense,
would smelt themselves should it come to that,
prefer hospitals and monasteries to Coliseum gore,
right hand quizzical before the left,
such is the pilgrim's flippant way,
first the destination, then count your change,
clanking coins reverberate to heaven—
spendthrifts for God—
tithing is meant for babies.

14. Mark 12:41–44.

Opposites Attract[15]

Opposites attract:
extrovert, introvert,
intuitive and rational
(Jungian schematic),
covalent bond.

North-south poles,
positron, negatron,
matter and anti-matter,
merger ignites:

Perfectionist flogs happy-go-lucky,
liberal locked under ball and chain,
irreligious hemmed in by prayer and piety,
generous at odds with stingy counterpart.

Androgyny? psyche union?
flame enveloping the candle?
oxygen dissolved in liquid hydrogen?
Monophysite heresy! a poet's Erewhon!

The best we can hope for is synchronized love,
two individuals temporarily one,
live and let live in a bipolar universe,
fantasies tempered by simple common sense,
the rose with its thistles, the ox still has its gore.

Romance insufficient, it takes willpower,
sex lasts only five beatific minutes,
a good cook maybe half an hour—
slug it out figuratively or one's negated the other.

15. Matthew 19:4–6.

Marriage, God's own institution,
sacramental grace the grease that makes it go,
viscosity thickens, the coefficient of friction on the rise,
despotic "I's" shudder in a ball-and-socket joint,
man rips it to shreds, but God can mend it twice as strong.

My God—No Miracles for Me?[16]

The pagan statues fall when the Christ-child passes,
clay sparrows come to life,
nurse Salome's hand withers,
my God—no miracles for me?

Can the Virgin be assumed?
Brother Francis heal the wolf and wren?
Peter's shadow sanctify the leper?
and I—all zeros for my score?

Alchemists grind on Aristotle's pebble,
magicians pull rabbits out thin air,
biologists snap babies from cervix tubes,
presto! no instant formulas for me?

Moses took on the whole house of Pharaoh,
Joshua—Canaanite bestial degradation,
Gideon—an army of Midianite storm troopers,
and I—not suited up in battle gear?

Mules speak, trees walk,
demoniacs rent themselves a pigskin,
a lamb with a sword stuck down its throat,
and me—no emblem or insignia?

You are a queer sort—
granting exuberance to some,
ahistorical accretions to another,
nein, gar nichts, kein etwas for the rest.

16. Luke 6:17–19.

If they brush aside the Son,
will dead Lazarus entice the crowd?

For Pascal[17]

"Ainsi nous ne vivons jamais, mais nous espérons de vivre."
—Blaise Pascal[18]

We never really live, we just intend to,
all mistake shadows for substance,
silhouettes for luminous details,
as in a dream we're fooled into believing
success can be achieved by simple sleight of hand.

Our most awesome decisions
are thwarted by timid fears, irresolution,
we move forward only after a backhand shove,
spend the day haggling and trading,
devising "What if" scenarios,
"Alibi" is our most constant companion,
"Duplicity," our truest friend.

We perceive the world through our teachers' lens,
should we discover that one true talent, then world watch out!
meanwhile, we picture ourselves in a hundred
    Shakespearean roles,
accepting laurels and wreaths,
when we haven't memorized the lines of a butler,
if the curtain is raised, we fly,
apologizing before we soliloquize.

17. Luke 12:19–20.
18. Pascal, *Pensées*, 90.

Near the atolls of our knowledge
lie troubling reefs and lagoons,
we're discovered stashing our acorns in collapsing trees—
surely God will overlook, forgive—
meanwhile, we dance on polished, frictionless glass,
at each major crossroad are mired in ambivalence,

Graze for a while in the most verdant spot,
become bloated from a surfeit of candy,
lambast our neighbor's minutest flaws,
yet never grow weary of extolling our own peculiar virtues . . .
if the day had twenty-six hours,
if there weren't so much pressure from family or competitors;
instead of jettisoning ballast, we wallow in all that's unreal.

The Wicked Chafe[19]

The wicked chafe like the proverbial reed,
like a banging shutter left open in a midwinter's squall,
wobble and jerk, zigzag like a hockey puck,
meander into oxbows, detour through Vanity Fair—
voluptuous Marlene Dietrich to soften our resolve,
King Midas and Horatio Alger to replace the Christ,
an oakleaf and the bays to lull our soul to bed.

In the whirlpool of living there's no time for life:
an infant, a game, an amusing occupation,
a hobby, a craft, a bewitching pastime.
Bipeds chase the ball or hare,
why, it's the very sport of kings!
Religion, too, is honeycombed with false passageways,
near the truth enlightened devils cluster—

Bareboning the creed, loosening the commandments,
or substituting their own faddist taboos.
In the hierarchy Faustian bishops unleash their delusions;
in congregations demagogues surface via vox populi;
a sect shrouds itself in supplemental revelation,
re-consecrates a pagan mentor, apotheosizes a quack.

The narrow gate is ever open,
but the well-watered thoroughfare draws the crowds
—in the hurdy-gurdy excitement, gratification is now.

19. Matthew 7:13–14.

I've Fallen[20]

How often have I fallen—
O Lord, you know that finite number—
placed my ballooning self before another,
if I could but abacus count.

Gone off like some floppy-eared prodigal,
rooting for scrumptious husks among the swine,
stilled my clanging conscience
with a winding, scholastic argument,
pretended to be deaf and dumb and blind
till you stung my shuttered eyes
with a cascade of illuminating tears.

Why should I admire that iridescent peacock
or soothe that simmering grouse?
demons have contorted, tattooed my torso and limbs,
imps zeroed in like vultures and pecked at my exposed joints.

I've flaunted eccentricities like a talk show run-at-the-mouth,
cracked the mold for newfangled deviances,
tittered at Everyman's impure passions,
kept counsel with a coterie of disingenuous flatterers,
then walked off with an archrival's trophies and ribbons
and thought that macabre enough revenge
for this world's rabid plagiarism.

20. Luke 15:13.

Exponential Sin[21]

Fruit-flies multiply faster than I can count,
so my sin in an exponential way;
as Linnaeus charted all taxidermy forms,
so Deuteronomy made a Sears Roebuck of human vice.
Before I wake my dreams will distort your tic-tac-toe
into hodgepodge grays,
until the harvest moon, buttonweeds will choke legumes.

I fast and pray until my Gadarene swine rush like legionnaires,
every photon exposes dungeons I've denied,
from every tincture that heals, bleeds a fresh red wound,
"What's the use," cried Isaiah, "except my lips be sealed?"

Forgive, forgive, forgive, till thou art sore,
O Lord, I have another score,
I confess acid disobedience,
stucco thoughts and felicities,
sporting words, unshaven tongue,
memories and concupiscence a mile from grace.

Except I close myself like nuns and speak through iron grills
(all vows are temporary), I whimper before that Winding Bobbin
in Easter disarray—a scarlet Mary Magdalene—
while that other Mary wafts perfume.

O Christ, gibberish and lies taint all these words;
every hour, drenched in sin, would I cry;
will you putty this cracked pot
to room a holy guest within?

21. Matthew 6:12–13.

And out my pores
gush tenderness and joys,
pop my cap,
so all can sniff—
pristine, dormant jugs are shelved.

Kyrie Eleison[22]

Kyrie eleison,
too often I've known what was right to do
but never tried,
buried my head in the safe sand,
while all about hurting, sobbing, screaming voices
reached out with desperate hands.

Christ, cover my torrential sins.
My talent, I've hidden from carping eyes,
then I've nearly strangled those audacious enough to disagree;
stretched the plastic truth, told fluid, hard-to-mop-up lies;
murmured against stern authority figures, bowed down
   before a golden calf;
lacked communal commitment, truly been afraid;
caused innumerable brothers and sisters to stumble and fall.

Christ, stop this blazing contagion.
I've fed my palate on smooth, comforting illusions,
manipulated and tricked those I couldn't persuade,
boasted in what chance had wrought,
raised up your blood-red banner, a two-ton cross,
let my wick simmer down and die,
missed untold sapphire opportunities.

Jesus, don't lose patience with this, your hesitating Thomas,
for Satan has desired to crush him with a single blow.
Plead, plead your vicarious merits before the high court,
remembering how this frame is loess, dust.
I've struggled against, resisted your Holy Spirit,
fallen asleep during a critical watch,

22. Luke 18:9–14.

toiled all night—fishless, then returned home dejected,
    with an empty net,
blabbering, "Show us the Father,"
"Explain to us the meaning of this parable."

Christ, my all, I put on the altar,
then I've surreptitiously sought to yank it back again,
certain that I know better
than the One who formed and kneaded this dough.
Forgive my tenuousness, skepticism; break my marble heart,
as I lay weeping over piffles, toys, distraught concerning
    tomorrow's manna,
when there's a fabulous new country to explore.

To what shall I compare this damburst mercy?
Surely no Judas could be impervious to its tsunami waves.

Something That Was Lost[23]

Something that was lost has been found
and I can hear the angels rejoicing,
whether it's sheep, keys or a coin,
the band is striking up golden ditties,
there's reminiscing, hugging, toasting,
speech gushes out as from a broken spigot,
the headman has killed the choicest calf
to make potlatch for the prodigal.

Meanwhile, we lying Cretans form a revolving circle,
like damned souls who walk in the futility of their desire;
we're immersed in viscous tears, near to drowning,
all avenues have been cut off by incessant loathing.
The saved lift up their heads and blink,
climb a bright and shining ladder,
tread upon the heads of scorpions and adders,
their ascetic forms almost ethereal.

For God is shaking the foundations and they're still trembling;
those who believe themselves sick are more likely to recover,
while those who clutch at patent panaceas
may end up more choleric than when they began.
To retrieve your lost bearings, enter a maze without a compass,
perceive that inherited maps may be rigged, passé,
that every shortcut is an untenable conceit,
then freefall into the lap of God.

23. Luke 15:8–10.

I Am . . .[24]

I am the coin that was lost,
the prodigal who ventured forth and squandered a fortune,
the foolish virgin left holding an oil-less lamp,
the publican who kept crying out with that mantra
    from the heart.

I am the trembling house built on quaking sand,
the wheat choked by usurious tares,
the naysaying son who later relented,
the talent which was hid and matured not one percentage,
the sheep who wandered off and fell down a crevice,
the debtor forgiven much who loved even more.

I am the priest who passed opposite the bleeding victim,
the blind man who followed his *starets* into a ditch,
the fig tree cursed for puny, shriveled-up fruit,
heartless Dives moaning over carefree Lazarus,
the merchant who sold all for one gleaming pearl,
the mustard seed which blossomed into a huge desert canopy,
the blinking beacon set upon a high, holy hill.

I am one from whom an unclean spirit has been banished,
only to become refuge to seven more vile than its predecessor.

24. Matthew 12:43–45.

Hands Defiled[25]

Why do your disciples eat with hands defiled
when the tradition of the elders forbids ceremonial uncleanness?
They rinse not the outer cup, profane the Sabbath,
set aside the sages' commentaries,
pursue God without encrusted, cumbersome intermediaries,
Hasidic feast with him heart-to-heart.

25. Mark 7:1–8.

The Mystic Whale[26]

Jacob's ladder shoots up
from Bethel to the Iona Cross,[27]
I'm already dizzy and my feet
are but five inches off its base.
My soul peeps out its sensual cage,
my intellect stuck between science and fantasy,
my clanging heart tolls purification.

Let the darkness stand
for this pre-Adamic space.
Seal up the Third Eye with gauze.
Revoke the charter of self-preservation.
The Beloved saws off each peg
in a metaphysical frenzy.
The void we know
and of that we cannot speak.

Seven tiers extending through Seven Edens:
the Logos Ineffable,
an Auditory Vision;
is this the enchanter's Dulcinea
or can God broadcast in Pidgin allegory?
The summits are jagged
and the pits deeper than all Tartarus—
who goes risks his sanity.

From the smoking cloud,
even Moses was forced to descend;
Jesus, too, was transfigured but an hour.

26. Matthew 17:2–3.
27. Thompson, "The Kingdom of God," 257.

There dragons and serpent schools swim
beside the squid that unhaired Jonah.
Go lower your buckets: land a mystic whale.

My Friend Lazarus[28]

My friend Lazarus has fallen asleep,
I go to awaken him with a supernatural kiss.

28. John 11:11.

To a Neo-Evangelist[29]

Come on out, Lazarus,
and rejoin our corporeal fray,
you've a post-mortem opportunity
to whistle and prove yourself a tuneful gallant,
so off with that specter-thin frown,
as if you alone had undergone
death's menacing tentacles and claws,
felt deprived of all but a tincture of God's mercy,
tell us your metaphysical tale.

Yet don't be abashed
if friends won't sound trumpets, host commemorative dinners,
since resurrections disturb our homespun civility
and we feel more at home with what's quantifiable, known,
instead of vague forebodings, shudderings of immortality;
to see you so recently smelling of the tomb
unnerves us, there are doubts we can't evade—
yes, we hanker after some former, comforting dispensation,
before God upped the ante.

We're happiest in clouds, since fog is our natural habitat,
endless sitting room speculations and high squabbles,
but to be in your incandescent, glowing presence—
well, what excuse does a neo-evangelist allow?
We desire fence-sitting postponements, hesitating perhaps,
for decision-making requires weighty considerations,
    pangs of research;
so, come on then, take up your previous, jovial self,
for this newborn earnestness and ardor is most unbecoming,
your sense of urgency just plain obtuse.

29. John 12:9.

Lift Up Your Drooping Knees[30]

Lift up your drooping knees,
be fervent with your fingers,
cuff God with a two hundred-volt whack,
address him in the Savior's name.

Besiege his honor with seventy-five petitions an hour,
doused in faith, ask Hur and Aaron's
aid, arm-twist angels till their blessing
bursts upon your head, give
the rosary a spontaneous whirl.

Abba, Abba, the spirit groans,
Teknon, Teknon, echo our molecules,
confessions, thanksgivings, and unmitigated praise,
absolution and clemency.

Christ above, Christ below, Christ *in medias rēs,*
   Christ the lever, Christ the fulcrum, Christ the center of gravity,
      Christ the yeast, Christ the dough, Christ the fiery oven.

Christ the sermon, Christ the parable, Christ the miracle play,
   Christ the rose, Christ the thorn, Christ the chlorophyll,
      Christ the tiger, Christ the chameleon, Christ the beluga whale.

Christ the integer, Christ the fraction, Christ the infinite series,
   Christ the anvil, Christ the crowbar, Christ the yardstick,
      Christ the body, Christ the soul, Christ the interface,
Christ the child, Christ the apprentice, Christ the man come of age.

---

30. John 14:13–14.

Be still my God and hear me pray
in languages known and neo-Pentecostal gibberish,
like a shopworn monk,
fill up my ballast tanks with Hours.

Perfume my intercessions with the blood of sheep,
stretch a mediator across the intergalactic bridge,
tilt Fate's die in my direction,
hide an Easter blessing inside each adverse egg.

May I have your attention, please,
am I a publican or a Pharisee?

They're Burning Heaven with Their Tears[31]

They're burning heaven with their tears,
scorching the pearly gates with loud and incessant pleas:
"Cast down the pretender!"
"Tear open Dives's taut purse strings!"
"Halt the invader's madness!"
"Restore to us our hemorrhaging sister!"
like a crack, elite band of commandos,
who handle the numen more gingerly
than a vial of nitroglycerine,
yet are not gun-shy before that Los Alamos accelerator.

The evil one's tipped arrows
are doused by that most potent of anti-toxins: faith;
as warriors who march victorious over unseen, debilitating legions,
they use the force of their mouths to pry open that celestial fortress—
transcendence breaking out in rumblings of immanence—
if only Abraham could pinpoint ten righteous men,
Aaron and Hur prop up Moses's drooping hands,
Peter and John screw up their eyelids for one intercessory hour,
heaven might still intervene and restore the balance spring
     toward equilibrium.

To be sure, they're storming heaven as though it were the Bastille,
razing worldly delusions under the inverse banner
     of contemplation.

31. Luke 18:1–8.

The Song of a Gardener[32]

I have determined, yes!
not to let the day sun scurry round its circuit
without one flower opening,
without some humble bee depositing his pollen,
without a shimmer of yellow or red.

I have determined bounty will surpass frugal leanness,
aesthetics will transcend base functionalism,
kindness will extend far beyond our bounden duty
and love will characterize my deeds.

But when I peer out—I discover no silver lining,
        no Ptolemaic epicycles,
        no upward evolving human race,
no providential symmetry of good.

Only LSD confusion,
a helter-skelter jigsaw puzzle
with a few missing pieces lost,
misfired pellets,
hieroglyphs that can't be read.

The world is far more chaotic
than certain French philosophers surmised,
I see trouble, toil, famine, and starvation,
picturesque lavas engulfing populations.

Clouds that soak as well as sprinkle,
tares standing side-by-side with corn,
yes! I would pluck out every noxious plant,
gently lie each weed upon its back.

32. Matthew 13:3–9.

But my horizon is just a few degrees, my sensitivity pretty narrow,
thus I have determined to make diversity a goal,
to nurture flowers in burgeoning profusion
to replenish the widest possible sperm bank.

On Honoring God[33]

Which honors God the more—
a steeple set among New England maples
or an auditorium full of clapping charismatics?
a Romanesque crypt
or a stained glass Madonna?
the Word of God preached or a layman taking Eucharist?

And which is more conducive to spiritual growth:
Byzantine icons or Quaker barrenness?
The Book of Common Prayer or extempore speech?
mysticism or acts of charity?

I think God more tolerant
than our denominational prejudices.
So purge, whip, excommunicate
eccentrics, dissidents, foreigners—
inquisition begets sweet innocence.

Or is my anger less righteous than my love?
Do I hate just those heresies I have spurned?
Since when did coercion convert one soul?
The devil arrives with hatchets and chains,
but God comes robed in incarnate frailty.

33. Luke 9:49–50.

"Please Accept My Apologies"[34]

My wife is about to give birth,
I have an appointment I simply cannot break,
there are fields to plow before the rains come,
I have guests to entertain, relatives to visit,
I must consult my analyst before any upsetting move,
I'm far too depressed to appear in public,
besides, I have nothing to wear,
let me first set out on my honeymoon
    and partake of the nuptial couch,
I'm engaged at a rather critical juncture in the research,
in six months I'll be a millionaire,
I've an old score to settle,
there's both a wake and a funeral to attend,
by the by, who else will be there?

I'm not much for socializing,
and what's the *real* agenda?
you scratch my back, of course I'll reciprocate,
I haven't any means of transportation,
what's the forecast—you know my allergies?
I don't have any handmade gifts to bring,
I'm not worthy of your table,
I should discuss this further with my spouse,
all right then—maybe next year,
is it formal or informal attire? and what's on the menu?
I may have lost the invitation,
there are a few loose ends to tie up (and bars to frequent),
sure, I'll do my best.

34. Luke 14:15–24.

Keep Awake[35]

I stand by the door
holding up a placard for all late-comers:
"Full Up. No Admittance"
—in the shape of a foolish virgin.

35. Matthew 25:1–13.

Willful Rejection[36]

The guest book of heaven
has many erasures.

36. Matthew 22:2–8.

The Entry into Jerusalem[37]

O prisoners of hope,
he ambled down those cobblestones
on the foal of an ass,
waving through his plastic bubble
    —the crowds, a mocking interlude
    "to fatten you up with friendship"
    like a New Guinea cannibal.

So many will-o'-the-wisp associates,
fairweather flag-wavers,
pepsodent-polished smiles
flinting up their machetes the minute you turn your back
    —what pompom bespangled splendor,
    press-the-flesh hypocrisy,
    Judas cheek-kisses.

Like Gene Autry at the Rose Parade,
you Bozo-crash through the bass drum
with your train of Big Ten can-can girls,
pep rally cheers for the miracle man
    —before pubescent girls pull off your rock concert clothes,
    Las Vegas plays blackjack for your stage prop crown
    or the Met auctions off your Gethsemane portrait.

Next time you'll know better
than to accept our accolade.

37. Matthew 21:8–9.

The Lord's Supper[38]

Do this until we sup again,
   drink of the chalice
and chew the starchy wafer,
   savor my flesh,
blow bubbles in my corpuscles,
   erupt the philosopher's rock
with the keys I to Peter gave.

Nineteen hundred and eighty genuflections since *Urmensch*'s folly,
   anagogic acts steeped in Eleusinian ritual,
bar the laity from this sheer accident?
   or am I manifest only where two or three
and the cassocked priest appear?
   contrite hearts I desire
or Mount Sinai would have thundered with amulets.

The harvest, an emblem of the celestial banquet,
   blood on the chattel's doorpost
smeared ubiquitous about the altar,
   except I bleed,
the Hebrews are God's bastard race,
   Yom Kippur, a penumbra,
the ark, an intermediary booth.

Thus the magnet drags
   just the lodestone foreordained,
better not to exit from the womb
   than to detain your rabbi
for an ingot of lead,
   so discern me now, my *agape* guests,
'else feast with Judas in another place.

38. Luke 22:19–20.

Meditations on Paschal Friday[39]

The pain comes,
but it oozes in slow,
like the prickly acids
in our ligaments and tendons
—eased with regular exercise—
the heart sputters, the brain stops,
arthritic agony.

Forsaken beyond all sentient life,
he hangs between point and counterpoint,
hope and despondency,
suspended between a curse and blessing.
Were you there
when they scorned him to the tree,
when they maligned, stripped, and manhandled our King,
when they squelched that healing lantern,
thumbscrewed God's best?

I cough in blood,
I spit out blasphemy,
I sing off-tune,
I shuffle towards *kakothanasia*,
bodies broken on altars far from love,
wine spilt by the tormentors of Job,
crushed cartilages, singed synapses,
blanched bones, resurrection dry,
peace rent in half,
in lowly pomp I ride in the caravan "Despair."

39. Mark 15:34.

An Exercise for Ignatius[40]

Let me not be numbered among these drunken transgressors
who taunt and jeer the accused under his iron load,
nor let me squat beside those gaming legionnaires
who squabble over the bloodstained cloak of Joseph
anxious to cast that dream-disturber into an unmarked cistern.

Might I not fall back, retreat or equivocate
when Judas implants that fingerprint kiss,
nor hold high the lantern of betrayal for Temple cutthroats
    and thugs
who consent to inglorious flagellation/scourging,
nor bleat like the orchestrated sheep for release of
    that butcher Barabbas.

Oh, would that I cast not the tie-breaking vote
in that ill-conceived, nefarious, mock Sanhedrin
agitated by conflicting testimony, accusations of blasphemy,
calling down upon Mt. Ebal whirlwinds for millennia
    and inevitable diaspora
for cutting off the prophet's limbs, cleaving God's very heart
    in two.

May I not be found among Herod's counselors eager
    for some conjurer's tricks,
nor stand aloof like Everyman from all apparent collusion
    with evil,
stopping up my ears to the prisoner's pleas and groans,
bending the law as if it were a compliant wagtail.

---

40. Luke 23:55–24:10.

May I rather saunter alongside these pious, grieving women
who bear spices and ointments to the sepulcher of the Paschal lamb
anxious to lance and cauterize the glaring wounds of
one who intermittently bleeds new Cana wine, offers up his body
    in Emmaus loaves,
might I be jubilant as a bell which never stops clanging
    this wondrous news.

The Crucifixion[41]

Earth has claimed its thirteenth victim;
the hunter aims at his despised foe
on a hill called Calvary—
humankind twitching on a dissecting board,
whirling vortex of an anti-world,
sacred nexus of two colliding planes,

Shrieking spectacle where angels stand aghast.
Two shots fired into the sacred canopy—
paradise transferred from Hades to the third heaven;
remorse lost in canyons almost too deep for the grace of God,
echoing and re-echoing light years from yesterday
in a million stillborn tomorrows.

A time warp now two thousand years long,
who can save this blighted star?
Shall space convulse in
inverse proportion to the first bang?
Will the cosmic vacuum suck in
both planets and asteroids without distinction?

Shall homeostasis be restored by its creator
in an evolutionary millennium or two?
Or will dry ice freeze out the warts and blemishes
and Eden be restored in a single hour?

I saw Christ scampering up the Cosmic Pole,
whisper the sounds of birds and mammals
and be received into glory at the Triune Festival Day.

41. John 19:17–18.

It is the earth's fatal crime
that seeing they do not see
and hearing they act confused,
as if the left hemisphere were waging war against the right,
bilateral symmetry gone awry in an ambidextrous universe,
corpus callosum snapping in an electrical overload,
myriads of sputtering circuits crying distress.

Split atoms keep regrouping again,
if only King Chronos would stop ticking away,
the *noosphere* drained of regressive ions,
where molecules are measured in parsecs
and life systems fail from the bitter cold,
O Jesus of the galaxies.

Here divides all reality
into *Lēthē* and *Zākar*,
the axis splintering our existence,
Stoic and antinomian condemned under the same natural law,
existentialist and presuppositionalist begging for mercy,
where even saints stand on merits they've never earned.
Will this be where I lay my burden down
or will it be the first set in an infinite series?

Can a hybrid being, half-unicorn, half-Phoenix,
annul the history of sorrows?
Can a juxtaposed Time redeem you and me?

Or, damn it all, will the Peripatetic teach again at his academy,
and Krita Yuga roll around for the umpteenth time
as untarnished as the very first dawn?
Will protein chains be transfigured into ameba,
and virtuous cows take human form?

If the dead are not raised,
we are still in the womb:
earth, water, fire, and air,
de-materialize our illusions
and give substance to our form.

Concerning Who Were the Real "Christ-Killers"[42]

It's not so important
who killed him—
Caiaphas, Pilate, Longinus's spear,
his own disillusioned, capsized heart.

First he begged to be delivered
from his father's bitterest cup;
later, recovering his resolve,
he set out like a jubilant martyr
for prophet-slaying Jerusalem.

In the upper room he commanded Judas
to hurry up with his shekeled kiss;
then impetuous Peter drew out his crusading sword,
until Jesus cured that belligerent zeal.

Calumniators rose up like rapid-fire guns,
yet couldn't agree on one sticking accusation
before Jesus pronounced his own blaspheming verdict;
Pilate puzzled over one lamb-deaf and silent.

Christ could have called twelve legions of angels
to rescue him from the *bēma* of fools;
so the guilt that incendiary mob called down
should be spread among all the world's descendants.

If we were upright, conscientious and pure,
never stumbled before the law,
sought God with eager, spontaneous hearts,
all might theoretically go scot-free;

42. Matthew 27:24–26.

but Eve was seduced,
Adam ate of the tempting pear,
and our solidarity with their misfortune
is repeated on every newscast.

The climax isn't
the public spectacle—a slave's horrid crucifixion—
but in that mysterious, unfathomable time before the world
    was conceived,
when the slain lamb volunteered
to undergo the pangs of Triune separation.

In that bleakest hour
he bore our punishment, our cure
(imperfection deserving estrangement from the holy);
it was a frightfully heavy load,
heavier than Hercules bore at Gibraltar,
heavier than starvation, rape and pillaging—
insipid instruments of torture—
for all these Jesus knew
and never shirked their tolerable weight.

But to experience the horror of the unknown,
the flaming gap between Lazarus and Dives—
God's wrath for every evil, every sin—
was infinitely more painful, devastating, final,
so all we need do now is to repent
and accept the lawgiver's full, unmerited reprieve.

That's what's important:
who's crucifying him now,
when salvation's work is in toto compleat.
For to some, time has stood still, lo these many years,
those who refuse to acknowledge his atonement
are urging the procurator on

to their second, more lasting death,
while Jesus pleads his oblation for all
—must he (God) suffer twice?

Don't Cry, Mary[43]

Don't cry, Mary,
he's interceding now,
John, behold thy matriarch,
Peter, let Beelzebub grind you into diamond powder,
    haunting hosannas,
    hail three malefactors and his scoffing kinsmen,
        a bone-shaking screech,
        a temple-rent heart,
        an anesthetic sponge,
        a mangled rosebush crown,
        a roulette table, a centurion who converts,
the latest ecstatic to adorn Salome's platter.

Don't cry, Mary,
he's going and he isn't coming back, unless you take him liter'ly,
Thomas, put out your doubting limbs and soothe his bleeding brain,
Judas, hang your sorrows on the forgiving tree,
    ungrateful lepers,
    seventy who left,
        a thief handed Eden on a silver spoon,
        scarlet wooden pegs,
        a nameplate in three spangled tongues,
        Longinus's spear puncturing his side,
        spicy ointments, a ghost harrowing limbo,
catch the water and the blood in a Eucharistic basin.

Don't cry, Mary,
he's in a better place,

43. John 19:26–27.

Pilate, be baptized in a finger bowl,
Simon, bear your own cross awhile,
   "save us all" taunts,
   lacerated dreams,
      Satan gleeful—maybe forty hours—
      Friday's casket, *Sonntag's* disappearing act,
      a sealed boulder hurled into space,
      hallucinating women—testimony invalid—
      a Gennesaret fish fry,
Adam's bloody skull, a serpent choking on an apple.

Don't cry, Mary,
he's almost glorified,
Sanhedrin, take back your verdict,
twelve, fulfill his final wish,
   Cleopas's *epistrophē* vision,
   five hundred witnesses standing all at gaze,
      matter-energy reunion, a gown of immortality,
      the glint of martyrdom, rivalries/contention,
      Messianic suffering, typological hermeneutic,
      feed my lambs with the manna that endures,
      a Pelican soaring from a frozen land,
a last appearance to acquit the chief prosecutor's soul.

Resurrection Morning[44]

On a chilly Easter morning
we went to lay our spices and ointments down,
in the Judean twilight, half-dream, half-dawn,
Hades bobbin standing before us like a monarch cocoon.

We wept to see the gardener,
a rock as huge as a Yap coin,
we shuffled like wet bulb thermometers,
envisioned St. Demetrius slaying that gladiator,
strange, turbulent thoughts darkened our hearts.

A second chaos is come again,
by devout men he was carried to his grave,
morning is far wiser than afternoon eclipsed,
the red knight to his fair red queen,
and all was prophesied of old.

II
As dumb as any migrating flounder,
we were straying, veering left,
the high priest we beheld with his twelve flashing stars,
the new Adam in whom all power dwells,
fearfully we ventured beyond the Gentile/women's court.

The predatory worm is soon devoured,
Pilate's machinations come untwined,
the Suffering Servant climbs to Sheol and returns,
so twang we out Magnus Annus and the spring.

44. Luke 24:1–3.

(Should I, who am lying on my back,
not the sky god see,
how are you lying on your belly
to witness Apollonius's rebirth?)[45]

III
Many a year from now
firecrackers and alleluias will recall
that it was women who first rejoiced,
and all tears were blotted on his sleeve.

In his car drawn by unicorns, blind Cupid ascends,
we Shulammite maidens follow like gazelles,
Enoch is translated, David's branch is sawn,
like newly engrafted buds we stretch and yawn.

Tell Peter, tell John,
we walked and a third was in our midst,
scales fell, Scriptures burned inside our hearts,
theophanies raged up and down the Emmaus road,
Jesus just paid rent on Gordon's tomb.

Let the whole world know
death is but a door.

45. Adaptation of an Ashanti proverb.

Since Christ Has Gone[46]

Since Christ has gone,
our hands are wet
with broken bubbles,
love is cramped, fled
to some distant, uncivilized shore.

We gladly endured parables
(harsh) and sayings (mysterious),
if our Teacher provided diagrams
(clarifying) and interpretive equations.

We closed our gaping mouths
before provisions multiplied,
demoniacs sitting as calmly
as you or I, the weak unburdened
and made glad, the congenitally-deformed,
paralyzed, bleeding, dying
—instantly and without relapse—
recuperating.

When we launched our rafts
into the cruel gale, we grew
afraid, then were struck with wonder,
while John's disciples fasted
and self-inflicted pain,
we ate and drank our bellies full
at the exuberant bridegroom's
inviting table, offered
leftovers to passing Gentiles.

46. Luke 24:50–51.

We observed the word of forgiveness
stifle evil, gratitude come back
more manifold than Abraham's descendants;
during those three-and-a-half years
humanity cheered the zealot,
bread-giving Messiah, then like Herod
turned a stone ear to beatitudes
and talk of "spiritual" riches.

We learned of Roman styles
of execution, tales of apocalyptic
lamentation, bickered amongst
ourselves for unfair position,
having left all—families, businesses,
villages we knew better
than the wrinkles on our faces.

So you've gone off,
ascended in a friendly cloud
in some tangible/intangible shape
—our hearts have stopped—
to fill the world with your evangel
and jagged sayings, we'll need
an inkling of your continued presence.

Otherwise, we'll return, forlorn
and unappreciated, to the stale,
rotting, desperate lives we've all led,
a stubborn, intractable people
in a resolute, unyielding land.

Christ Is Our True Hercules[47]

Christ is our true Hercules[48]—
snapped the gorgon's neck,
cleansed the Augean stables
of heathenish superstition,
slew the seven-headed hydra,
sin's loathsome manifestation.

He fired upon those brazen birds
inhabiting success' highest rung,
stole the golden apples
drenched in fond immortality,
subdued giants, vanquished man's cannibal heart,
his cloak, the three-looped knot of perpetual virginity.

At the wedding feast he butchered his mother's fears,
by wielding the lion's club of his power
terrorized both Pluto and Cerberus,
led a host of blood-soaked captives past Mount Calpe,
strangling the twin serpents: lust and greed.

Christ lifted up the veil of Alcestis,
rejected vice and embraced the wisdom of Minerva,
unbound Prometheus, set the house of Jupiter on edge,
offered himself up on Isaac's pyre,
was finally borne aloft on a chariot fit for gods.

47. Matthew 12:28–30.
48. This poem uses as a springboard an entry in Alexander Ross's *Mystagogus Poeticus*.

Baptism[49]

Renounce the devil you white-washed robes,
dunk your transgressions in a translucent fount,
like a dyslexic reverse your state,
throw a millstone about your stench,
rise up as a soaking neophyte,
trick Belial with a *metanoia* stunt.

I believe in one monotheistic constant
and one primate emanation from his holy name,
a reliqued cross and a ravished tomb,
that faith is the cord that can set it all right;
I pledge allegiance to a Pentecostal gale
and worship with my sisters of the second order.

Now do the angels roar their approval,
since hell has sprung a pinhole leak;
salvation is gratis, God bought it wholesale.
Wash away the phosphates Adam bequeathed,
strip off encumbrances and swim like a pike,
jump out of your stale tank into an ocean of love.

49. Matthew 28:19–20.

Consider the Lilies[50]

Consider the lilies
arrayed in their orange finery,
more resplendent than Solomon's processional gown,
they neither sweat nor work themselves into a fever,
but partake freely of the benevolent air and soil.

Their morning sacrifice is the purest nectar,
in the evening they bend their heads in secret prayer,
their trumpets blow silent, wind-borne praise,
just as Asaph's brethren jump to and fro
about the ark in a continual tumult.

Their arching stalks turn skyward
toward that luminary appointed to christen the day,
opening their spotted petals
to drink in and seize a full measure of ultraviolet vitamins,
they solicit in seductive, see-through attire,
underground feelers absorb iron and copper,
chloroplasts once invisible turn emerald green.

I note the fields of happy, un-ulcerated flowers,
remember man's haste to accumulate perishable treasures,
hour after ludicrous hour
spent on ever more successful preservation techniques,
while piled up grain dries on its surface, molds underneath.

War, famine, and pestilence annihilate a lifetime
of misspent energy and vaunted ambition—
such have their heartbroke reward—
while laughing lilies in the midsummer's breeze
are contented and serene as Franciscan friars.

50. Matthew 6:28–34.

Soul-Fishing[51]

Have I brought along perky bait,
is today's oxygen/Fahrenheit level invigorating,
am I casting out shiny, wiggling lures
along nutrient-rich banks and shelves,
testing a full complement of hooks and weights,
isolating each consecutive variable: the line, the knot, the sinker,
and, if need be, mothballing my original bamboo stick?

But am I truly committed, resolute
to troll unstintingly,
encapsulating the Gospel
in a sublime, albeit apologetic form,
so if the cultured despisers
start to nibble,
I can jerk on my bone hook,
haul in a few wayward minnows?

Yet shall I dare to flaunt the trenches and canyons,
go bottom-fishing after those recalcitrant ones,
or remain content to dragnet off a stationary dock,
bobbing after the scrawny, floating, throwaway,
never experiencing the pristine joys of a deep-sea evangelist?

51. Mark 1:16–18.

Recommended Reading

Religious Anthologies

Atwan, Robert, George Dardess, and Peggy Rosenthal, eds. *Divine Inspiration: The Life of Jesus in World Poetry*. Oxford: Oxford University Press, 1998.

Atwan, Robert and Laurance Wieder, eds. *Chapters into Verse: Poetry in English Inspired by The Bible, 2 Volumes*. Oxford: Oxford University Press, 1993.

Curzon, David, ed. *The Gospels in Our Image: An Anthology of Twentieth-Century Poetry Based on Biblical Texts*. San Diego: Harcourt Brace & Company, 1995.

Curzon, David, ed. *Modern Poems on the Bible: An Anthology*. Philadelphia: Jewish Publication Society, 1994.

Davie, Donald, ed. *The New Oxford Book of Christian Verse*. Oxford: Oxford University Press, 1981.

Gardner, Helen, ed. *A Book of Religious Verse*. New York: Oxford University Press, 1972.

Levi, Peter, ed. *The Penguin Book of English Christian Verse*. New York: Penguin, 1984.

Works Cited

Emerson, Ralph Waldo. "An Address." In *The Portable Emerson*, edited by Mark Van Doren, 54-55. New York: Viking, l965.

Erasmus, Desiderius. "The Handbook of the Militant Christian." In *The Essential Erasmus*, edited by John P. Dolan, 58. New York: New American Library, 1964.

Kay, George R., ed. *The Penguin Book of Italian Verse*. Baltimore, Maryland: Penguin, 1958.

Panofsky, Erwin. *The Life and Art of Albrecht Dürer*. Princeton: Princeton University Press, 1955.

Pascal, Blaise. "No. 168." In *Pensées*, edited by Jacques Chevalier, 90. Paris: Librairie Générale Française, 1962.

Pelikan, Jaroslav. *Jesus Through the Centuries*. New Haven: Yale University Press, 1985.

Ross, Alexander. "Mystagogus Poeticus." In *Classical and Christian Ideas in English Renaissance Poetry*, edited by Isabel Rivers, 31. London: George Allen & Unwin, 1979.

Thompson, Francis. "The Kingdom of God." In *The New Oxford Book of Christian Verse*, edited by Donald Davie, 257. Oxford: Oxford University Press, 1972.

Wesley, John. *The Journal of the Rev. John Wesley, A.M.: Volume 2*. Edited by Nehemiah Curnock, 202. London: Epworth Press, 1938.

Scripture Index

www.ingramcontent.com/pod-product-compliance
Lightning Source LLC
LaVergne TN
LVHW021617080426
835510LV00019B/2626